The Aviation Notebook

BAe/McDONNELL DOUGLAS

HARRIER

Stewart Wilson

Airlife
England

AV-8B Harrier II BuAer 162951 of VMAT-203, the US Marine Corps training squadron. The unit was the first to receive the AV-8B in January 1984, this photograph was taken in April 1987.

Contents

Copyright © 2000 Stewart Wilson and Wilson Media Pty Ltd
First published in the UK in 2000
by Airlife Publishing Ltd

First published in Australia by Wilson Media Pty Ltd

British Library Cataloguing-in-Publication Data
A catalogue record for this book is available from the British Library

ISBN 1 84037 218 4

Production and design: Gayla Wilson and Wendy Wilson,
Special thanks to Australian Aviation. Colour profiles by Juanita Franzi.

Printed in Australia

Airlife Publishing Ltd
101 Longden Road, Shrewsbury, SY3 9EB, England
E-mail: airlife@airlifebooks.com
Website: www.airlifebooks.com

Towards V/STOL

The date was 1 May 1982, and the occasion was significant. On that day, nine Royal Navy Fleet Air Arm Sea Harrier FRS.1s led by Lt-Cdr A D Auld carried out a gun and bomb attack on Falkland Islands' Port Stanley airfield at the start of the battle to regain the British sovereign territory from the invading Argentineans.

Later on the same day the Sea Harriers were blooded in air-to-air combat when they claimed an Argentinean Mirage and Canberra. By the end of the conflict they had scored 23 confirmed victories in the air for no losses in that area of operation, while RAF Harrier GR.3s had also made a very large contribution to the campaign in the ground attack role.

The concepts which had started to be developed in the design offices of Hawker Aircraft and Bristol Aero Engines 25 years earlier had been proven. The Harrier was much more than just a crowd puller at air shows.

1957 was not a good year for British manufacturers of military aircraft. That was the year of the infamous Defence White Paper which proclaimed that the days of manned combat aircraft were over and that missiles would take their place. The document threw the British aircraft industry into chaos because it resulted in the cancellation of many important combat aircraft projects.

For a company like Hawker, whose bread and butter had for decades been supplying fighters to the Royal Air Force, it was a potential disaster. The company was at the time developing the P.1121 supersonic air superiority and strike fighter with its own funds and was building a prototype. By the first half of 1958 it became clear that officialdom had suddenly lost its previous enthusiasm for the aircraft and it was abandoned.

Hawker still had the Hunter in production at the time but nothing to follow it. In early 1957 the company had launched a study under the direction of chief designer Sir Sidney Camm for a vertical takeoff and landing (VTOL) jet aircraft designated the P.1127. There had been experimental VTOL aircraft developed before but some relied on the use of separate lift and propulsion engines and others on a tail sitting launch attitude, neither of which had much if any potential as practical, operational aircraft.

The Wibault Factor

Meanwhile, a French aeronautical engineer and an American Colonel were about to have a substantial influence on the P.1127. Michel Wibault had been involved in the design of several French aircraft and his company had built airliners during the 1930s. In April 1956 he took his concepts for

Second generation Harrier. GR.5 ZD202 was used as a testbed for the Pegasus 11 Mk.61 with which it first flew in June 1989. As the F402-RR-408A, the engine powers USMC AV-8B Plus aircraft.

a vertical takeoff aircraft called *Le Gyroptère* to the French Air Ministry, which showed little interest.

As Wibault was convinced the VTO aircraft which were launched from a tail standing position were impractical for operational use, *Le Gyroptère* was a 'flat riser', one which took off and landed in a normal attitude. Importantly, Wibault also rejected the idea of separate lift and propulsion engines, instead using a single jet engine which discharged its exhaust gases into four centrifugal blowers and then four linked nozzles which could be rotated through an arc from horizontally aft to vertically down-wards - in other words, vectored thrust. A normal jet pipe in the rear of the aircraft also provided forward thrust.

Wibault's ideas gained a glimmer of hope in early 1957 when he approached the Paris office of the NATO Mutual Weapons Development Team (MWDT), an organisation set up to foster the development of selected European military projects by providing financial assistance. Most of the money was supplied by the USA, and the MWDT was already involved with Bristol on the Orpheus turbojet for the Fiat G.91 lightweight fighter for supply to European Air Forces.

MWDT's Colonel Bill Chapman suggested that Wibault take his ideas to Bristol. He did, meeting the company's technical director Dr Stanley Hooker, who immediately realised the implications of what he was seeing. Bristol had been looking for a way into the VTOL engine business but Rolls-Royce (into which Bristol was later absorbed) held the necessary patents for lift engines, a concept Hooker was not overly enamoured with.

Here was Bristol's chance to steal a march on Rolls-Royce with a new concept which Hooker and his team recognised as being a potentially better solution to the problems of achieving practical VTOL flight.

The Bristol Pegasus

Within weeks, Bristol's engineers had designed a powerplant applying Wibault's principles but in simplified form, eliminating the Frenchman's centrifugal blowers and the complex gearboxes and shafting. Called the BE.52, the engine utilised the core of the Orpheus driving a forward extension shaft to a fan (taken from the Olympus) with its exhaust discharging through a pair of rotatable nozzles and a normal rear jet pipe.

This quickly evolved into the BE.53 Pegasus with four nozzles and no aft jet pipe. The fan was moved back to the forward end of the engine and rotated in the opposite direction to the compressor to eliminate gyroscopic effect. The inboard portion of the fan functioned as a supercharger for the

The essential ingredient in the success of the Harrier - its Pegasus vectored thrust turbofan. This example is a Pegasus 11 Mk.61 (F402-RR-406A) from a Spanish Navy TAV-8B.

compressor and the outboard portion drove a large mass flow of cold air through ducts on each side of the engine and then through a pair of nozzles. The hot gases from the rear of the engine were similarly discharged.

The Pegasus 1 produced about 8,000lb (35.6kN) thrust and was bench tested for the first time in August 1959.

Bristol also developed the low speed and hovering stabilisation system (or reaction control system, RCS) which would be applied to the P.1127/Harrier. This utilised engine bleed air directed to downwards facing control valves in the aircraft's nose, tail and wingtips and was controlled by the pilot through instinctive stick movements.

Bristol took its engine concepts to Hawker in mid 1957, the manufacturer making substantial changes to existing P.1127 concepts in order to accommodate the new engine. There was the general feeling that a major breakthrough in combat aircraft design was about to be achieved.

Unfortunately, this came at the same time as the 1957 Defence White Paper, with the result that official British interest in the P.1127 was non existent. Bristol, however, managed in June 1958 to secure finance from the MWDT to cover 75 per cent of the Pegasus' development costs but the airframe remained a Hawker private venture for the time being.

The first P.1127 (XP831) photographed in early 1963 when it was fitted with inflatable bag-type intake lips, one of several intake configurations tested. XP831 operated from a ship (the carrier HMS *Ark Royal*) for the first time in February 1963.

Hawker P.1127

The P.1127 design evolved into an overall configuration which was very similar to the Harrier as it eventually emerged, although structurally and in detail it had little in common with the production model. The major features were there - the anhedral wing (originally a type of delta with unswept trailing edges), the tandem undercarriage with outriggers, the four swivelling nozzles, the RCS and of course the Pegasus turbofan engine. The tailplane originally lacked anhedral while the intake lip design changed considerably between the first appearance of the P.1127 and the production Harrier.

Hawker authorised the building of two P.1127 prototypes at its own expense in mid 1958 and after some lobbying an operational requirement to cover the concept (GOR.345) was issued in April 1959. It would be another six months before the company received any government financial assistance with the awarding of a parsimonious contract to carry out further design work.

It is perhaps significant to note that there was enthusiastic and practical US involvement by this stage with NASA undertaking the testing of free flying and transonic wind tunnel models for the P.1127 programme.

Finally, on 22 June 1960, the British Ministry of Supply issued Hawker a contract covering two prototypes under Experimental Requirement (ER) 204D and allocated the serial numbers XP831 and XP836. A further four prototypes were subsequently ordered.

XP831 was delivered to Hawker's Dunsfold facility for final assembly in July 1960 and rolled out on 31 August for initial engine runs and weighing. The flight engine was a Pegasus 2 developing 11,300lb (50.39kN) thrust, just sufficient to lift the P.1127 vertically in the tethered hovering that would make up the first part of the flight test programme.

The big day was 21 October 1960 when chief test pilot Bill Bedford lifted the P.1127 very briefly for its first and very unstable flight. The aircraft was tethered so it couldn't rise more than about a foot, had been stripped of anything non essential to save weight and carried only 35imp gal (160 l) of fuel for the same reason.

An interesting sidelight was that Bedford had one ankle in plaster on that historic day, the result of a road accident. He would have been unable to fly a conventional aircraft safely but for this occasion he was issued with the probably unique medical clearance, "Fit civil test pilot, tethered hovering only"!

XP831 performed 21 tethered hovers over the next five weeks before being set free, while the first conventional wingborne flight was performed on 13 March 1961 after a rolling takeoff. The second P.1127 (XP836) first flew on 7 July 1961 but was lost the following December when one of the front fibreglass cold nozzles detached, leading to asymmetric thrust, a loss of control and the necessity for Bill Bedford to eject. The front nozzles were consequently made of more durable metal.

From late September 1961 the first transitions from the hover to conventional flight were performed and the flight envelope expanded with numerous detail changes made to the aircraft along the way. Powerplant development also continued with the 12,000lb (53.4kN) thrust Pegasus 2 available in the first half of 1961 and the 13,500lb (60.0kN) thrust Pegasus 3 in March 1962. Mach 1 was exceeded in a shallow dive for the first time in December 1961.

October 1961 saw the start of short rolling takeoff trials, this method of departure extremely significant for the future operational use of the aircraft. Although the ability to takeoff vertically was important, to do so obviously required a power-to-weight ratio well in excess of unity, thus seriously limiting the fuel and/or weapons load which could be carried.

XP980 was the fifth P.1127, first flown in May 1963 and the first to introduce the definitive anhedral tailplane.

Using the nozzles to provide horizontal power early in the takeoff roll and then rotating them downwards when the wing began to develop some lift provided a short takeoff run and much greater weapons/fuel carrying capability. With the fuel load reduced and weapons gone, a vertical

landing could be made. This was the mode (STOVL) in which the fully developed Harrier mostly operated and its usefulness as a combat aircraft was enhanced accordingly.

The first of the four additional P.1127s (XP972) first flew on 5 April 1962 and was joined by XP976, XP980 and XP984 between then and October 1963. XP890 introduced the definitive anhedral tailplane and streamwise wingtip fairings while XP984 was the first to be fitted with a swept wing.

By then, the P.1127 had became a Hawker Siddeley product following the grouping together of Hawker, de Havilland, Folland, Armstrong Whitworth, Avro and Blackburn under that title in accordance with British Government policy. Vickers, Bristol, English Electric and Hunting were also amalgamated as the British Aircraft Corporation.

Kestrel

The P.1127 concept was quickly proving to successful and began to attract international interest, this confirmed in May 1962 when the US, British and West German governments announced they were jointly funding an order for nine evaluation aircraft to be called the Kestrel and given the designation FGA.1 by the RAF.

The aircraft would be operated by the Tripartite Evaluation Squadron based at RAF West Raynham, Norfolk and introduced new design developments including the swept wing which had appeared on the final P.1127, a taller fin, longer front fuselage, a camera in the nose and provision to carry underwing fuel tanks. A wider span tailplane was fitted from the second Kestrel.

Power was from a 15,200lb (67.6kN) thrust and substantially redesigned Pegasus 5 fed by air from revised intakes. The first Kestrel (XS688) flew on 7 March 1964 at a time when it was not regarded as having any production future due to plans for the supersonic P.1154 (see below).

The last of the Kestrels flew in March 1965, by which time the Tripartite squadron was well established, the P.1154 had been cancelled by the British Government and development of an operational version of the

Four Kestrels of the US, UK and West German Tripartite Evaluation Squadron with XS693 in the foreground. The first Kestrel (XS688) flew in March 1964 and the aircraft was an important step in the development of the operational Harrier.

P.1127/Kestrel for the RAF approved. Suddenly, the Kestrel and its trials assumed greater importance.

By February 1965 the Kestrel fleet had recorded 545 flying hours, 1,343 V/STOL takeoffs and landings and hundreds of routine transitions. Speeds of over Mach 1 had been achieved in a dive and at the other end of the scale the aircraft had been flown at 61kt (112km/h) sideways and 26kt (48km/h) backwards. Night operations had also been carried out.

The Tripartite squadron disbanded in November 1965, after which six of the Kestrels went to the USA for Tri-Service trials under the designation XV-6A. The other two survivors (one had been lost) remained in the UK for development work associated with the forthcoming P.1127(RAF) production version.

Supersonic P.1154

NATO became interested in V/STOL aircraft in 1961, issuing specification NBMR-3 for a combat aircraft capable of flying at Mach 1.5. Earlier in the year, Hawker had instigated its P.1150 project for such an aircraft, powered by a developed version of the Pegasus called the BS.100 with much increased maximum power due to plenum chamber burning, a process which injected fuel into the normally 'cold' front nozzles and burnt it in the discharge air.

The P.1150 was notably larger than the P.1127 but used the same basic principles. From there the concept developed into the P.1154 with a 33,000lb (146.8kN) thrust version of the BS.100 to meet the NATO requirement. This it did, and was declared 'technical ' winner of the competition in 1962. However, national sensibilities proved impossible to ignore and the rival Dassault Mirage IIIV/Balzac (which used eight Rolls-Royce lift engines and a Turboméca Atar propulsion engine) was politically favoured. These political issues proved too much for those making the decisions and this potentially very important programme was dropped.

Hawker Siddeley then attempted to develop the P.1154 to meet a draft joint RAF/RN requirement for a multirole aircraft in a common airframe. The RAF wanted a single seat strike aircraft and the RN a two seat carrier based interceptor and the differences were too great to easily resolve. A version powered by two vectored thrust developments of the Rolls-Royce Spey was even studied for the RN. The inter-service squabbling was continuing when the new British Labour government under Harold Wilson was elected in October 1964. It quickly solved the problem by cancelling the P.1154 when construction of a prototype was already underway.

With benefit of hindsight it's probably just as well the highly complex and expensive P.1154 was cancelled when it was because attention was able to be returned to the P.1127/Kestrel, further development of which was immediately approved.

Artist's impression of the supersonic P.1154. This highly advanced V/STOL design was proposed to meet NATO and then RAF/RN requirements but was cancelled in early 1965.

Harrier GR.1/3

Even though the British Labour Government's cancellation of the super-sonic P.1154 in January 1965 had been a blow to Hawker Siddeley and the British aviation industry generally, it did result in the 'consolation prize' of allowing development of the Kestrel into a fully operational aircraft for the RAF. A new Air Staff Requirement (ASR 384) was issued to cover what was initially known as the P.1127(RAF) and later Harrier GR.1.

Based around the more powerful 19,000lb (84.5kN) thrust Pegasus 6 Mk.101 engine with increased mass flow, water injection and numerous detail design improvements, the P.1127(RAF) represented a 90 per cent redesign over the Kestrel with substantial fuselage and wing structural modifications to withstand the rigours of its planned low level ground attack and close air support role. A ventral air brake was also installed, replacing the previous system which used the main undercarriage door for this purpose.

The wing had tip extensions, vortex generators and fences added (detachable ferry tips which increased the span were developed but rarely used in service) and the undercarriage was redesigned with its energy absorbing capacity increased substantially from 13,000lb (5,897kg) while descending at 8ft (2.4m)/sec in the Kestrel to 16,000lb (7,258kg) at 12ft (5.4m)/sec.

The P.1127's original 'constant bleed' reaction control system was wasteful of engine power and replaced by a more efficient 'on demand' system in the production aircraft, while the Pegasus 6's greater appetite for air resulted in redesigned and mechanically variable intakes with and the addition of six (later eight) 'blow in' auxiliary inlets around them for use in the hover and at low speeds.

Operational equipment included a Marconi two-axis (later three-axis) autostabilisation system, a Ferranti inertial nav-attack system, Smiths Industries head up display (HUD - the first British military aircraft to be so equipped), an optically projected moving map display on the main instrument panel and a 70mm oblique camera in the nose. No radar was fitted.

The P.1127(RAF) could carry two 30mm Aden cannon (or a reconnaissance pod) under the fuselage and four underwing hardpoints were fitted to carry a combination of weapons and fuel tanks up to a theoretical maximum of 9,000lb (4,082kg), although 5,300lb (2,404kg) was the practical maximum on the Harrier GR.1.

(Opposite) One of the development batch Harrier GR.1s performs a rolling takeoff from a wet flight deck during shipboard trials. The first of six development GR.1s flew in August 1966 and the last in July 1967.

Harrier GR.1 XV782 of 4 Squadron RAF based in Germany overflies the Möhne Dam, one of the targets of the famous 'Dambusters' raid by Lancasters in 1943. The RAF kept a Harrier presence in Germany for nearly 30 years.

A development batch of six pre production aircraft (XV276-XV281) was ordered in February 1965. The first of these flew on 31 August 1966 and the last in July 1967. The aircraft had meanwhile been named Harrier GR.1 and an initial order placed for 60 production aircraft.

(Below) A Harrier GR.3 at the hover. This upgraded version introduced Laser Ranging and Marker Target Seeking (LRMTS) equipment in a reprofiled nose, a more powerful Pegasus 103 engine and radar warning receivers in the tailcone and leading edge of the fin. XZ131 of 4 Squadron was one of 40 a new production GR.3s; others were converted from GR.1s.

The first production Harrier GR.1 (XV738) flew on 28 December 1967 and five others were in the air by the end of 1968. The Harrier Operational Conversion Unit (No 233) took delivery of its first aircraft on 18 April 1969 and operational service with No 1 Squadron at Wittering began two months later.

Delivery of the initial GR.1 production batch had been completed by April 1971 and subsequent orders took the total to 78 (plus the development aircraft), the last of them flying in January 1972.

The public got its first real exposure to the Harrier in May 1969 when two aircraft (XV741 and XV744) from No 1 Squadron participated in the *Daily Mail* newspaper's Trans-Atlantic Air race between the centres of London and New York and back. The Harrier crews avoided lengthy road journeys to and from their aircraft from the race's starting and finishing points by departing vertically from a coal yard near London's St Pancras railway station and after several in-flight refuellings, landing vertically on a Manhattan Island wharf.

The importance of this was not winning the event but demonstrating the Harrier's operational flexibility and the fact that it didn't need conventional runways. The Harriers won the eastbound leg but were beaten by a fired up (literally, thanks to sustained use of afterburner) Royal Navy Phantom crew on the return journey, utilising helicopters to get to and from their aircraft. But it was the remarkable sight of the Harrier 'Jump Jet' (as it had been dubbed by the press) operating from the middle of two major cities which captured the public's imagination.

The air race Harriers were fitted with a fixed refuelling probe and the detachable extended ferry wing tips in one of the very few times they were used.

GR.1A: Designation applied to 40 Harrier GR.1s retrofitted with the 20,500lb (91.2kN) Pegasus 10 Mk.102 engine, allowing a 1,000lb (454kg) increase in maximum takeoff weight. The conversions were performed as the original engines became life expired and needed to be changed. The upgraded electrical system developed for the USMC's AV-8As was also subsequently installed.

Another German backdrop for a 4 Squadron Harrier GR.3. Converted GR.3s were delivered to the RAF between 1973 and 1976 and the first new aircraft flew in January 1976.

GR.3: Further engine power growth via the 21,500lb (95.6kN) Pegasus 11 Mk.103 and operational equipment enhancements resulted in the Harrier GR.3, this built for the RAF in both new and converted forms. The Pegasus 103 was similar to the F402-RR-402 specified by the USMC for its AV-8As and featured a re-bladed fan to increase mass airflow, water injection cooling of the high pressure turbine blades and improved combustion characteristics.

Externally, the GR.3 differed from its predecessor in have a longer and reprofiled nose housing Ferranti Type 106 Laser Ranging and Marked Target Seeking (LRMTS) equipment which allowed the aircraft to designate and detect ground targets and also provided a search capability. The result was much improved bomb delivery accuracy, this and the increased maximum takeoff weight of 26,000lb (11,794kg) enhancing the Harrier's combat effectiveness.

The GR.3 also received a passive radar warning receiver (RWR), this involving the mounting of antennae in the leading edge of the fin and in the tailcone to provide 360deg coverage. Most surviving RAF Harrier GR.1/1As (61 aircraft) were converted to GR.3 standards between 1973 and 1976.

The 84th and last Harrier GR.1 had been delivered in 1972 and in 1974 a further batch of 12 new aircraft was ordered and built to GR.3 standards, the first of them (XZ128) flying on 9 January 1976. Further batches of 24 ordered in 1978 (delivered April 1980-June 1982) and four in 1982 after the Falklands War brought the new build GR.3 total to 40.

The RAF began winding down Harrier GR.3 operations in 1988 as the GR.5 started to come on line. The final 'official' flight was performed on 29 June 1994 by ZD670 (the last GR.3 built) by No 20 (Reserve) Squadron.

(Opposite) A Harrier GR.3 of No 233 Operational Conversion Unit takes off during an air show demonstration. The OCU and its successor, 20 (Reserve) Squadron, has been the RAF's Harrier training unit since April 1969.

HARRIER GR.1/3 and AV-8A

Powerplant: GR.1 - one 19,000lb (84.5kN) Rolls-Royce Pegasus 6 Mk.101 vectored thrust turbofan. GR.1A/early AV-8A - 20,500lb (91.2kN) Pegasus 10 Mk.102/F402-RR-400. GR.3/AV-8A - 21,500lb (95.6kN) Pegasus 11 Mk.103/F402-RR-402. Internal fuel capacity 630imp gal (756 USgal/2,865 l) in five fuselage and two integral wing tanks; two underwing drop/ferry tanks each of up to 330imp gal (396 USgal/1,500 l) capacity.

Dimensions: GR.3 - wing span 25ft 3in (7.70m) standard or 29ft 8in (9.04m) with ferry tips; length 46ft 10in (14.27m); height 11ft 6½in (3.52m); wing area 201sq ft (18.7m²) standard or 216sq ft (20.1m²) with ferry tips.

Weights: GR.3 - operating empty 13,535lb (6,140kg); max takeoff 26,000lb (11,794kg).

Armament: Provision for two 30mm cannon in underfuselage pods; four underwing hardpoints for max 5,300lb (2,404kg) ordnance.

Performance: GR.3 - max speed (clean) 642kt (1,189km/h) at low level or 573kt (1,062km/h) with typical external load; time to 40,000ft 2.4min from vertical takeoff; service ceiling 51,200ft; takeoff roll at maximum weight 1,000ft (305m); combat radius with 4,400lb (1,996kg) load 200nm (370km) lo-lo-lo or 360nm (667km) hi-lo-hi; max ferry range 1,850nm (3,427km).

AV-8A Harrier

It is part of Harrier mythology that the US Marine Corps' order for the aircraft resulted entirely from the unannounced arrival of two of its pilots at the Hawker Siddeley chalet during the 1968 Farnborough Air Show, requesting a copy of the pilot's notes and to fly the aircraft. Two weeks later both men flew a Harrier and an order resulted.

The reality was slightly different. It is true that Colonel Tom Miller (later the USMC's Chief of Staff Air) and Lt-Col Bud Baker did present themselves at Hawker Siddeley's chalet and did fly a Harrier two weeks later, but their arrival was expected and it wasn't as if the Americans had been previously unaware of the aircraft or disinterested in it. After all (and as explained in the opening chapter), US money had contributed to development of the Pegasus engine through the Mutual Weapons Development Programme (MWDP), wind tunnel testing had been performed in the USA and both the USMC and US Air Force had been closely involved in the evaluation of the Kestrel.

Further, the USMC had for some time been wanting an aircraft with the capabilities promised by the Harrier - deploying at the front line near the troops, capable of operating from land or ships with minimal logistical support and not requiring conventional runways or flight decks.

Miller and Baker completed their evaluations and reported back that here was the ideal aeroplane to meet the USMC's needs. From there things moved quickly. A US Navy test pilot team arrived in Britain in January 1969 to formally evaluate the aircraft and its positive results led to the Harrier's cause being taken up by senior and influential people within the service and the US Government.

As a result, funding was made available in the 1970 fiscal year appropriations for the purchase of an initial 12 aircraft (as the AV-8A or Harrier Mk.50 by the British) for the USMC as part of a declared intention to obtain 114 by the mid 1970s. This was ultimately reduced to 110 including eight two seaters. The money for the purchase came from the reallocation of funds which had been earmarked to re-equip two USMC F-4B Phantom units with upgraded F-4Js.

Conditions imposed on the order were that the aircraft was to be an 'in production, off the shelf' type with a very small number of modifications required to meet the USMC's needs, and that a substantial production content would be undertaken in the USA.

To comply with this, Hawker Siddeley and McDonnell Douglas signed a 15 year licence agreement in late 1969 which assigned the US company

This rear view of AV-8A BuAer 158390 (the seventh built) of USMC squadron VMA-231 shows some good underside detail. This particular Harrier was first flown in May 1971 and delivered to the USMC two months later.

The US Marine Corps ordered an initial batch of 12 AV-8A Harriers with deliveries beginning in January 1971. Apart from some minor equipment changes and the ability to carry Sidewinder AAMs, the AV-8A was similar to the British model.

'exclusive rights for the sale and manufacture of the Harrier and its derivatives in the USA, and agreeing to the mutual exchange of data and drawings on vectored thrust V/STOL configurations stemming from the Harrier during the same period.'

As it turned out, the US Government decided the cost of transferring AV-8A production across the Atlantic was too great for the relatively small number of aircraft involved and like all first generation Harriers, the AV-8A was manufactured at Hawker Siddeley's plant at Kingston in England. The Pegasus engines were also built in Britain and given the US military designation F402. A joint development agreement covering the Pegasus was signed by Rolls-Royce and Pratt & Whitney in October 1971.

Hawker Siddeley's licence agreement with McDonnell Douglas would have to wait a few more years before it would be fully exploited and have a profound effect on the direction of the Harrier programme.

The AV-8A differed only in detail from British GR.1A with US Navy/Marine Corps radios replacing the RAF equipment, the fitting of a weight-on-wheels switch to make weapons circuits safe when the aircraft was on the ground, and the changes needed to carry USN/MC ordnance including a pair of Sidewinder air-to-air missiles on the outer pylons. The nose mounted camera was retained.

Service experience resulted in the overly complex (for USMC operations) Ferranti inertial nav-attack system being replaced from the 60th aircraft by a simpler Smiths Interface/Weapons Aiming Computer (I/WAC) that was retrofitted to earlier aircraft. This formed what was known as the Baseline System which provided the necessary attack calculations and information for the pilot on the existing headup display.

AV-8As from the 90th aircraft had their original Martin-Baker ejection seats replaced with US built Stencel units as part of an overall policy to use local seats where possible and to introduce some commonality to the USN/USMC fleet.

The first AV-8A (BuAer 158384) flew on 20 November 1970 and deliveries of the initial batch of 12 began in January 1971. Subsequent batches ordered in 1971 (18 aircraft), 1972 (30), 1973 (30) and 1974 (12) brought total USMC AV-8A procurement up to 102, the last of them (BuAer 159377) first flown in December 1975 and delivered the following month.

The first 10 AV-8As were powered by the 20,500lb (91.2kN) thrust F402-RR-400 (Pegasus 102) engine due to the temporary unavailability

of the specified F404-RR-402 (Pegasus 103). The earlier aircraft were subsequently retrofitted with the more powerful engine.

One interesting aspect of USMC AV-8A operations was the introduction of the technique called 'VIFF' (thrust Vectoring In Forward Flight) in order to enhance the agility of the aircraft in combat. It was first tested on one of the XV-6A Kestrels in 1970 and later with AV-8As, producing improved sustained turn rates and what was described as 'eye watering' deceleration.

The Harrier already had a high power-to-weight ratio and excellent acceleration which took many pilots of conventional fighters by surprise. This in combination with 'Viffing' at appropriate times made the Harrier more than a match for many supposedly superior fighters, as air combat testing against F-86 Sabres, F-4 Phantoms, T-38A Talons and other aircraft in the USA and Britain proved.

In a dogfight, it was found that moving the nozzles forward into the vertical position could cause such rapid deceleration that a pursuing enemy aircraft would overshoot and find itself a target for the Harrier's weapons. Square turns and various defensive breaks were also possible by 'Viffing', these usually resulting in the Harrier taking the advantage in a dogfight.

AV-8C: The conversion of 47 AV-8As between 1979 and 1983 to an enhanced standard resulted in the designation AV-8C. The upgrade included fitting forward looking passive radar warning equipment on the wing tips, some of the lift improvement devices developed for the AV-8B, tail warning radar in the bullet fairing behind the fin, a flare/chaff dispenser in the rear fuselage, an on board oxygen generation system and upgraded radio.

The upgrade also included a service life extension programme (SLEP) which increased the airframe's life from 3,000 to 4,000 flying hours. The AV-8C (and remaining AV-8As) had been withdrawn from USMC service by the end of 1987.

AV-8S: The designation of 11 AV-8As for the Spanish Navy ordered via the USMC in 1973 (six aircraft) and 1977 (five). They were designated VA.1 Matador by the Spanish and Harrier Mk.55 by the British. Similar to USMC Harriers apart from their radios, the first example flew on 18 September 1975 and deliveries began in November of the same year. See 'Harrier Operators' chapter for further details.

A pair of AV-8As (BuAer 158390 and 158385 from the initial batch delivered in 1971) carrying the markings of USMC squadron VMA-231, the 'Aces'.

(Opposite) A lineup of Harriers belonging to the USMC training squadron VMAT-203 at Cherry Point. This mid 1980s shot shows four AV-8As in the foreground and three AV-8B Harrier IIs behind them during a time of transition from the old model to the new.

USMC AV-8As aboard the assault carrier USS *Saipan*, one of five 39,000 tonne ships in the *Tarawa* class commissioned between 1975 and 1980. Seaborne operations were and remain an integral part of the USMC's deployment of the Harrier.

Sea Harrier

Throughout its development, testing and early service, the Harrier's designers and marketing team had always envisaged a maritime role for the aircraft. While the US Marine Corps' AV-8As were operated both from ships and dry land, it wouldn't be until 1975 that an order for a dedicated carrier based version of the aircraft was announced.

The quest to develop a 'Sea' Harrier had begun while the P.1127 was still being developed in the late 1950s, Hawker clearly seeing the potential for a vertical/short takeoff and landing combat aircraft with naval application. The Royal Navy showed little interest but the US Navy did, this later translating into the procurement of AV-8As by the Marines.

The Royal Navy did begin to show more interest in the concept in the early 1960s after it had seen the P.1127's capabilities, but this interest transferred to the supersonic P.1154. Although its cancellation in early 1965 was regarded as a blow to Hawker and the British industry, it at least refocused attention on the subsonic P.1127 and its planned operational derivatives.

A Harrier (or at least a P.1127) operated from a ship for the first time in February 1963 when test pilots Bill Bedford and Hugh Merewether performed a series of vertical and short takeoffs and vertical landings in the first prototype (XP831) aboard the carrier HMS *Ark Royal*. Neither had any previous experience flying from ships and the sorties were performed with no difficulties. Further trials followed over the years from other British and foreign vessels - including from small helicopter platforms on conventional warships - these operations proving to be remarkable in the fact they were so 'unremarkable', simple and straightforward. RAF Harrier GR.1s also successfully operated from the carriers HMS *Eagle* and *Ark Royal* in 1970-71.

Several events combined to change the RN's thinking: cancellation of the proposed 50,000 tonne CVA-01 'super carrier' in 1966; the planned end of RN Fleet Air Arm conventional fixed wing flying from aircraft carriers and the retirement of the ships (this occurred in 1978); and the development of a new class of euphemistically named 'Through Deck Cruisers' (later 'Command Cruisers') ostensibly intended for anti-submarine warfare (ASW) helicopter operations but with an unobstructed flight deck. The colloquial 'Harrier Carrier' was quickly applied to the ships by those who could see what the RN was really thinking!

The class's lead ship, the 19,800 tonnes HMS *Invincible* was laid down in 1972 and launched in 1977. The year before construction of *Invincible* had begun, and determined to find a way of maintaining fixed wing flying,

XZ438 was numerically the first Sea Harrier FRS.1 but was the second to fly, in December 1978. It was used for trials purposes and is pictured here carrying a pair of Sea Eagle sea skimming anti-shipping missiles.

the RN requested development of a seagoing version of the Harrier GR.3 which could operate from the new ships. Hawker Siddeley was awarded a design study contract the following year, with 'minimum change' over the GR.3 a stipulation.

The new Harrier's primary role was specified as air defence with a 400nm (740km) radius of action at altitude; secondary roles were strike and ground attack against ships and shore targets plus reconnaissance with the capability of searching 20,000 square miles of sea in one hour at low altitude.

Design work was completed by 1973 but due to political uncertainties the decision to order what would be called the Sea Harrier FRS.1 (for 'fighter-reconnaissance-strike') was delayed and looked in doubt for a time. Finally, on 15 May 1975, and order for 24 aircraft was announced (three development and 21 production) with a further 10 added to the initial contract in 1978.

Crucial to the operational success of the Sea Harrier was development of the 'ski jump' ramp, developed in 1972 by Royal Navy engineering officer Lt-Cdr Douglas Taylor. Use of the ramp provided the aircraft with the ability to become airborne some 25kt (46km/h) slower than a conventional short takeoff, translating into a halving of the takeoff run or a 30 per cent increase in weapons or fuel load for a given weight. It also reduced the need for the parent ship to attain high into wind speeds for aircraft launches.

For the Harrier's pilot, the technique involved starting the takeoff run with nozzles pointing aft, launching off the ramp and immediately selecting 40deg nozzles down as the aircraft began its semi-ballistic trajectory. The nozzles were then gradually moved back, the aircraft transitioning to normal wingborne flight.

Sea Harrier FRS.1 XZ493 of the RN Fleet Air Arm's 801 Naval Air Squadron. XZ493 was delivered in January 1981 and served in the Falklands. The aircraft is flown here by Commander Nigel 'Sharkey' Ward DSC AFC, the CO of 801 NAS and responsible for three 'kills' in the conflict.

Official support for the ski ramp idea wasn't forthcoming until late 1976 and a ground based ramp was built with its angle variable between six and 20 degrees. The first test (at 6deg) was conducted by Harrier GR.1 XV281 on 23 August 1977 and the results were immediately impressive.

It was decided that the three new Harrier Carriers would be fitted with ramps - 7deg on *Invincible* (commissioned July 1980 after a delay caused by the late decision to include the ramp) and *Illustrious* (June 1982), and 12deg on *Ark Royal* (November 1985). The first two were limited to the lower (and not optimum) figure by structural and defensive armament considerations. The old fleet carrier HMS *Hermes* underwent a refit and had a 12deg ramp installed, it, *Invincible* and the Sea Harrier going on to prove the overall concept in the 1982 Falklands War.

(Below) Royal Navy Sea Harrier FRS.1s and RAF Harrier GR.3s flew side by side from the carriers *Invincible* and *Hermes* during the 1982 Falklands War. This temporary and unplanned 'Joint Force Harrier' concept is now official British policy.

FRS.1: The major external difference between the Sea Harrier FRS.1 and the Harrier GR.3 was the completely new forward fuselage housing a cockpit raised by 11in (28cm) in combination with a more 'bubbled' canopy to improve pilot visibility and provide more equipment space underneath; and a reshaped folding nosecone housing Ferranti Blue Fox radar, a first for the Harrier.

Blue Fox was derived from the Sea Spray radar used in the Westland Naval Lynx helicopter and modified to operate in air-to-air and air-to-sea modes. The cockpit was upgraded to incorporate the multimode weapons system with a new Smiths HUD driven by a digital computer, this also functioning as a weapons aiming computer. Radar information was presented on a TV screen in the cockpit and the avionics were upgraded to include Doppler radar.

Under the skin, the Sea Harrier featured the replacement of many magnesium components with corrosion proof alloys while the Pegasus 104 engine was also corrosion proofed for shipborne operations with aluminium alloys replacing magnesium-zirconium major castings. Ferrous materials were coated with aluminium paint. A faster acting Martin-Baker Mk.10 ejection seat replaced the GR.3's Mk.9 and the wingtip reaction controls' power was increased. Remarkably, the weight penalty for 'navalising' the Harrier was a mere 100lb (45kg).

The Sea Harrier's primary armament options were the AIM-9 Sidewinder AAM and Harpoon or Martel ASMs plus the usual pair of 30mm cannon under the fuselage. A wide variety of other NATO ordnance could be carried.

Hawker Siddeley was merged into British Aerospace in January 1978. The first Sea Harrier FRS.1 to fly was XZ 450 - the first production aircraft - on 20 August 1978, ahead of the three development batch aircraft. Deliveries to the RN Fleet Air Arm's Sea Harrier Intensive Trials Unit (later No 700A and then 899 Naval Air Squadron) started in June 1979 and regular service began with No 800 Squadron in March 1980.

The initial production batch of 31 aircraft had been delivered by May 1982 as the Falklands War was in full swing. Further orders increased the FRS.1 production tally to 57, the last delivered in September 1988. It was withdrawn from RN FAA front line service in 1995, replaced by the Sea Harrier F/A.2.

FRS.51: The Indian Navy was the only export customer for the Sea Harrier, ordering an initial six as the FRS.51 in December 1979. Subsequent orders increased the number to 23. The first FRS.51 (the 34th Sea Harrier off the line) flew on 6 August 1982 and deliveries began in January 1983. Changes incorporated in the FRS.51 compared to the RN's aircraft were minor and included installation of a gaseous rather than liquid oxygen system, different radios and a primary armament of Matra R.550 Magic AAMs instead of Sidewinders.

Mk.80: Proposed export version of the FRS.1 with the Blue Fox radar replaced by Laser Ranging and Marked Target Seeking (LRMTS) equipment as on the Harrier GR.3 and optimised for the ground attack/close support role. Not built.

F/A.2: Late 1982 investigations into a Sea Harrier mid-life update resulted in the development of what was originally designated the FRS.2 and from May 1994 the F/A.2 (for fighter/attack). The new model would be created both by conversion of existing FRS.1 airframes and by new build aircraft.

Enhanced capability was incorporated by replacing the original Blue Fox radar with Blue Vixen multimode equipment (in a reshaped radome) with lookdown/shootdown, multiple target tracking and improved surface detection capabilities. A new integrated weapons/avionics suite and digital databus was fitted along with an updated cockpit with revised displays and hands-on-throttle-and-stick (HOTAS) controls.

The F/A.2 is capable of carrying new weapons including the AIM-120 Advanced Medium Range Air-to-Air Missile (AMRAAM), the BAe Sea Eagle sea skimming anti-ship missile and the ALARM air launched anti-radar missile. A 13.75in (35cm) stretch of the rear fuselage provides an extra equipment bay. The wing underwent some subtle changes including a reprofiled leading edge, the addition of a third fence and deletion of one of the 12 vortex generators.

The first converted F/A.2 (ZA195) flew on 19 September 1988 and a contract for the conversion of a total of 34 aircraft was awarded three months later. The first production conversion was delivered in April 1993 and the last in November 1997.

A contract for an initial 10 (later 18) new build F/A.2s was placed in March 1990 and the first example (ZH796) delivered in October 1995. The final aircraft (ZH813) was handed over to the RAF on 24 December 1998 as probably the last new Harrier of any version. According to some, it was also the last all British pure combat aircraft, discounting the trainer based Hawk 200.

Conceived as a mid life upgrade for the Sea Harrier, the F/A.2 was built new and converted from FRS.1s. XZ497 pictured here in the markings of 899 NAS was one of the converted airframes.

The Royal Navy received a total of 52 Sea Harrier F/A.2s (18 new aircraft and 34 conversions) between April 1993 and December 1998.

BAe SEA HARRIER

Powerplant: One 21,500lb (95.6kN) Rolls-Royce Pegasus Mk.104 (FRS.1) or Mk.106 (F/A.2) vectored thrust turbofan. Internal fuel capacity 630imp gal (757 USgal/2,865 l) in five fuselage and two integral wing tanks; two underwing tanks up to max 330imp gal (396 USgal/1,500 l) each.

Dimensions: FRS.1 - wing span 25ft 3in (7.70m); overall length (incl nose probe) 47ft 7in (14.50m); height 12ft 2in (3.71m); wing area 201sq ft (18.7m²). F/A.2 - length 46ft 5in (14.15m).

Weights: FRS.1 - operating empty 13,884lb (6,298kg); max takeoff 26,200lb (11,884kg). F/A.2 - operating empty 14,585lb (6,616kg); max takeoff 26,200lb (11,884kg).

Armament: Two 30mm cannon under fuselage; normally 5,000lb (2,268kg) ordnance on four underwing and two underfuselage hardpoints including air-to-air, air-to-ground and anti shipping missiles, bombs and rockets.

Performance: Max speed 635kt (1,176km/h) at sea level, 527kt (977km/h) at 36,000ft; max cruise 450kt (833km/h) at low level; combat radius (high altitude intercept) 405nm (750km); combat radius (low level attack) 305nm (565km); radius of action (reconnaissance) 525nm (972km).

Hawker P.1127 first prototype XP831 in February 1963 when it operated from a ship (HMS *Ark Royal*) for the first time.

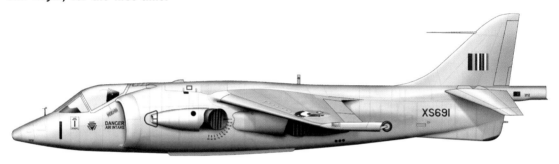

Hawker Siddeley Kestrel FGA.1 XS691 of the Tripartite Evaluation Squadron, RAF West Raynham October 1964.

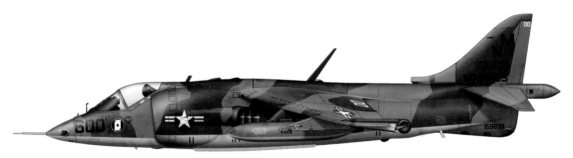

Hawker Siddeley AV-8A Harrier BuAer 159239 of VMA-231 'Aces' squadron USMC, embarked on the USS *Roosevelt*, Mediterranean late 1976.

Hawker Siddeley Harrier GR.3 ZD667 (the fourth last built) of 4 Squadron RAF, Germany 1990.

BAe Sea Harrier FRS.1 XZ457 of 800 NAS RN, Falklands War May 1982. Aircraft credited with four kills (three shown as fourth confirmed later), two each by Lt-Cdr A D Auld and Lt C Morrell.

BAe Sea Harrier F/A.2 ZE693 (converted from FRS.1) of 800 NAS RN, Operation Desert Fox over Iraq early 1999.

BAe Harrier GR.7 ZG862 (the last new build) of 3 Squadron RAF, mid 1990s.

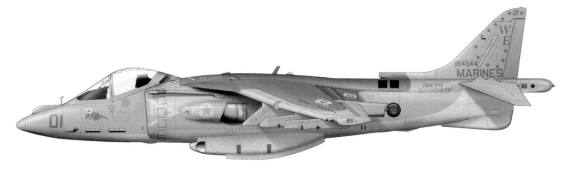

McDonnell Douglas AV-8B(NA) Harrier II BuAer 164544 of VMA-214 'Black Sheep' squadron USMC, mid 1990s.

Harrier II

In the wake of the late 1969 licence production and joint development agreement between Hawker Siddeley and McDonnell Douglas, the two companies began studies for a second generation Harrier in 1973. The studies were based around the new 24,500lb (109.0kN) thrust Pegasus 15 engine under the unofficial designation AV-16, the '16' symbolic of it having twice the capability of the AV-8A.

Although the first generation Harrier had proved the V/STOL concept to be successful, improved payload/range performance was needed and this was the motivation behind the AV-16. A larger wing was considered necessary in combination with a more powerful engine.

The problem was that the Pegasus 15's fan was of 2.75in (70mm) greater diameter than that of the Pegasus 11 used in the AV-8A and GR.3, this necessitating a redesigned and larger fuselage. The prohibitive cost of continuing development along these lines saw the AV-16 project cancelled in 1975 with the British Government withdrawing support due to budget cuts.

The two companies therefore went their separate ways for the moment, Hawker Siddeley investigating a 'big wing' for the Harrier which could be retrofitted to existing aircraft, while McDonnell Douglas pushed ahead with concepts for an enhanced Harrier which kept costs down by using the existing powerplant and basic fuselage structure.

It was at this point that the fundamental direction of the Harrier programme changed, with the American company starting to take the lead. When a Memorandum of Understanding between McDonnell Douglas and British Aerospace covering Harrier II production was signed in August 1981 the airframe workshare split (in terms of man-hours) was McDonnell Douglas (as prime contractor) with 60 per cent and British Aerospace with 40 per cent for USMC aircraft and 50/50 for RAF aircraft. Powerplant work was 75 per cent Rolls-Royce and 25 per cent Pratt & Whitney and final assembly of the aircraft was undertaken in both St Louis and Dunsfold.

Specifically, McDonnell Douglas built the wing, front and forward-centre fuselage (including the nosecone and intakes), underfuselage fences, forward fuel tanks and tailplanes for USMC and export aircraft; BAe was responsible for the rear-centre and rear fuselage, fin, rudder, reaction control system and the tailplanes of RAF aircraft.

But there was a long way to go before this happened. McDonnell Douglas pushed ahead with its ideas, based around incorporating a new, all composites, supercritical and one piece wing, taking advantage the extensive research into graphite epoxy and carbonfibre composites carried out by the Royal Aircraft Establishment at Farnborough.

McDonnell Douglas converted two AV-8As to YAV-8B configuration as aerodynamic prototypes for the Harrier II. The aircraft had the new wing, intakes and LIDs installed but not the redesigned cockpit area and lengthened rear fuselage.

BuAer 158394 was the first YAV-8B to fly, on 9 November 1978.

The new wing was of greater span and aspect ratio, had 15 per cent more area, reduced sweep (from 34deg to 30deg at quarter chord), was lighter, capable of carrying more fuel due to its increased thickness and was tailored to the USMC mission profile.

The Harrier II was the first production combat aircraft to use composites extensively. Apart from the wing, composites were also used in the tailplane, rudder, flaps, nose and forward fuselage. By weight, composites made up some 26 per cent of the structure.

The outriggers were moved from the tips to mid span to improve ground handling in tight spaces, larger high lift slotted flaps were fitted and the wing was able to have four hardpoints per side instead of the previous two, although USMC aircraft initially had only three.

The first of four full scale development AV-8B Harrier IIs flew in November 1981. Just visible here are the double row 'blow in' pressure recovery doors on the inlets, these only fitted to the development aircraft. Production AV-8Bs reverted to a single row of doors.

Other features of the Harrier II as it would emerge included larger air intakes; the fitting of lift improvement devices (LIDs) which were underfuselage longitudinal fences with a retractable dam between them, these trapping a cushion of air under the fuselage (adding the equivalent of 1,200lb/544kg lift) and also helping prevent the ingestion of gasses; a redesigned forward fuselage with raised cockpit and 'bubble' canopy; lengthened rear fuselage and revised tailplane.

When it entered service, the Harrier II would also feature the latest digital cockpit, avionics and aircraft and weapons management systems technology (much of it derived from F/A-18 Hornet practice) but no radar until the AV-8B Plus came along. Equipment included multifunction displays, hands-on-throttle-and-stick (HOTAS) controls, a three axis Sperry stability

augmentation and attitude hold system and a radar warning receiver. Design fatigue life without modification was 6,000 hours, twice that of first generation Harriers.

Formal US Government approval of the Harrier II was given in July 1976 and the aircraft designated AV-8B. Due to defence spending economies introduced by the Carter Administration following its election later in the year, the programme had to survive many attempts to have its funding cut before production started.

McDonnell Douglas meanwhile modified a grounded AV-8A (BuAer 158385) to include many of the AV-8B's physical features (with the new wing rendered in wood and metal rather than composites) and tested it in the NASA Ames Research Centre wind tunnel. It also converted two aircraft to YAV-8B flying prototypes (see below).

In Britain, efforts to develop a 'big wing' Harrier (the wing made of metal, not composites) with Leading Edge Root Extensions (LERX) continued under the designation Harrier GR.5. With only 60 aircraft required for the RAF, economies of scale finally became a major factor and Britain joined the USA in the Harrier II programme via the August 1981 Memorandum of Understanding.

YAV-8B: Two AV-8As (BuAer 158394/158395) were converted to aerodynamic prototypes for the AV-8B featuring the new wing, intakes and LIDs but not the redesigned forward fuselage/cockpit and lengthened rear fuselage. As the YAV-8B they flew for the first time on 9 November 1978 and 19 February 1979, respectively, but the second aircraft was lost in November 1979 after an engine flameout.

Flight testing of the YAV-8Bs revealed much greater drag than anticipated and therefore slower speeds. Modifications to the wing root fairing, intakes and underwing pylons helped little, but the despite this it was discovered the new aircraft would meet USMC payload/range, general performance, V/STO performance and fuel consumption

Deliveries of the AV-8B to the USMC began in January 1984. This one is operated by squadron VMA-331.

The AV-8B Night Attack variant is recognisable by the FLIR fairing on the top of the nose. All AV-8Bs from the 167th onwards (delivered September 1989) were completed as NA versions. This is the prototype (BuAer 162966), converted from a standard AV-8B and first flown in June 1987.

The AV-8B Plus represents a substantial leap in capability due to the addition of pulse-doppler multimode radar mounted in a reshaped nose. This is the prototype conversion, first flown in September 1992. Formerly BuAer 164129, it was given the new serial 165305 on conversion.

requirements. Consideration was briefly given to fitting the new wing and LIDs to existing AV-8As as a stop-gap.

AV-8B: By the time the MoU between Britain and the USA was signed in August 1981, production of the AV-8B for the USMC was already underway with components for the first aircraft manufactured in both countries.

The first of four full scale development (FSD) AV-8Bs (BuAer161396) was nearing completion at St Louis and recorded its maiden flight on 5 November 1981. The second and third aircraft (BuAer 161397/398) both first flew in April 1982, these introducing the leading edge wing root extension (LERX) developed by the British in order to meet RAF turn performance requirements. As originally installed, this was the so-called '70% LERX', smaller than the definitive versions.

The development batch aircraft also featured two rows of 'blow in' pressure recovery doors on the inlets but the second row was deleted on production aircraft when a revised intake ducting design made them unnecessary.

The fourth FSD AV-8B (BuAer161399) first flew in June 1984, McDonnell Douglas having meanwhile received authorisation to build an initial batch of 12 production AV-8Bs with a further 324 planned. The final AV-8B figure for the USMC was 232 including the FSD aircraft but excluding 30 new build AV-8B Plus models (see below).

The first production AV-8B (BuAer161573) was handed over to the USMC in January 1984 with the remainder of the initial batch of 12 entering service with training squadron VMAT-203 at Cherry Point between then and April 1985.

They were powered by the 21,450lb (95.4kN) thrust F402-RR-404A but the similarly rated -406A (Pegasus 11 Mk.105) with a digital engine control system and cooler running for increased times between overhaul came on line during 1985. From 1990, AV-8Bs were powered by the uprated 23,800lb (105.8kN) thrust F402-RR-408A (Pegasus 11 Mk.61). The first front line squadron to receive the aircraft was VMA-331 (a former A-4 Skyhawk unit) in January 1985.

AV-8B production (including the Night Attack version described below) had been completed by 1994 in favour of the AV-8B Plus. Exports were made to the Spanish Navy (12 as the EAV-8B/VA.2 Matador II) bringing production of the original AV-8B up to 244 including the Night Attack version.

AV-8B Night Attack: McDonnell Douglas was awarded a design definition contract for a night attack version of the AV-8B in late 1985. Originally known as the AV-8D, the designation AV-8B(NA) was finally settled on.

The AV-8B(NA) differed from the basic model in having forward looking infrared (FLIR) equipment mounted in a small fairing on top of the nose cone, a wide field of view HUD and night vision goggles for the pilot. Powerplant for all but the first few was the F402-RR-408A.

Other external features which marked the differences between the basic AV-8B and the NA version were flare/chaff dispensers on each side of the

upper rear fuselage and a longer ram air intake at the base of the fin. This was necessary to prevent the ingestion of hot debris from the dispensers.

AV-8B BuAer 162966 was converted to the prototype NA model, first flying in its new guise on 26 June 1987. All AV-8Bs from number 167 (BuAer 163853 delivered in September 1989) on were completed as Night Attack versions until the AV-8B Plus came on line.

AV-8B Plus: The Harrier II gained a major upgrading of its capabilities with the AV-8B Plus, this version combining the features of the AV-8B Night Attack with the addition of Hughes (later Raytheon) APG-65 pulse-doppler multimode radar in place of the angle rate bombing system (ARBS).

The new radar allowed substantially enhanced air combat capabilities including beyond visual range missile engagement. The number of underwing weapons pylons was increased from six to eight (the same as RAF aircraft) and new weapons carrying possibilities include the AIM-120 advanced medium range air-to-air missile (AMRAAM) plus Harpoon and Maverick air-to ground/surface missiles.

External changes over the basic AV-8B and NA versions include a reshaped nose for the radar and incorporation of the larger '100% LERX' as fitted to British Harrier IIs, albeit of a slightly different shape.

McDonnell Douglas and British Aerospace launched development of what eventually emerged as the AV-B Plus as a private venture in June 1987 under the working designation AV-8E. In September 1990 a Memorandum of Understanding between the USA, Italy and Spain was signed, allowing the latter two nations' industries a share of the work including local assembly of the aircraft they had ordered for their navies (see 'Harrier Operators' chapter for details). A USMC order was placed in December 1990.

The AV-8B Plus for the USMC has been supplied in both new build (30 aircraft) and converted forms with 72 of the latter funded and about 40

McDonnell Douglas built 30 new AV-8B Plus Harriers and by the end of 2000 the company (now Boeing) had delivered about 40 of the 72 funded conversions.

conversions completed by the end of 2000. At the time, the USMC was seeking funding to purchase additional rebuilt aircraft.

The conversion to AV-8B Plus standards requires a substantial remanufacturing of the aircraft including the incorporation of a new forward fuselage and reworking of the wing and undercarriage. It costs about two thirds as much as a new aircraft and its extent led to the USMC allocating new serial numbers to the rebuilds.

The prototype AV-8B Plus was converted from AV-8B(NA) BuAer 164129 and first flew in its new guise (as BuAer 165305) on 22 September 1992. Deliveries of new build aircraft to the USMC began in April 1993 and had been completed by the beginning of 1995.

GR.5: Due to Britain's delay in formally joining the Harrier II programme, the Royal Air Force became an operator of the second generation aircraft more than two years later than the USMC. Sixty examples of the initial Harrier GR.5 were ordered with the signing of the August 1981 MoU, these differing from the USMC's AV-8B in having some revised avionics, weapons management and general equipment, a different 25mm cannon installation plus two additional underwing pylons for the carriage of Sidewinder AAMs.

The other pylons were slightly redesigned to carry RAF-specific weapons (including the BL755 cluster bomb) and the wing leading edges, intake lips and windscreen were increased in thickness and strengthened for the RAF's stringent birdstrike requirement of being able to survive the impact of a one pound (0.45kg) bird at 600 knots (1,110km/h). Powerplant was the 21,550lb (95.8kN) Pegasus 11 Mk.105.

Deliveries of the Harrier GR.5 for the RAF began in July 1987. This head on view clearly shows the smaller Leading Edge Root Extension (70% LERX) fitted to some aircraft and the four underwing pylons per side.

The first Harrier GR.5 (ZD318) flew on 30 April 1985 and the first aircraft delivered to the RAF was ZD324 in July 1987. Brief operational service began the following year, replacing the Harrier GR.3, with most of the 43 aircraft quickly converted to GR.7s.

GR.5A: The last 19 Harrier GR.5s were completed as GR.5As, an interim standard incorporating the wiring and some other equipment to enable easy conversion to GR.7 standards.

GR.7: The definitive RAF Harrier variant to date, the GR.7 represents a substantial leap in capability. It is similar to the USMC's AV-8B Night Attack Harrier, featuring FLIR and provision for pilot night vision goggles. Other changes over the GR.5 include the installation of a colour (rather than mono) moving map display and from the 17th aircraft, a new '100% LERX'.

The first of 34 new production GR.7s (ZG471) flew in May 1990 and the final example (ZG862) was delivered to the RAF in June 1992. All surviving Harrier GR.5/5As (49 aircraft) were converted to GR.7 standards between 1990 and 1994 and since then it has been the sole single seat Harrier variant in RAF service.

Twelve GR.7s used to fly armed reconnaissance patrols over Kosova in 1999 were equipped with Vinten lightweight reconnaissance pods while others had thermal imaging and laser designating pods fitted to direct Paveway laser guided bombs to their targets.

GR.9: The designation Harrier GR.9 was originally used in 1989 for a proposed version powered by the uprated Pegasus 11 Mk.61, as fitted to the USMC's AV-8B Plus aircraft as the F402-RR-408A. The designation reappeared in 2000 for a planned GR.7 upgrade which would allow the aircraft to carry the new generation of 'smart' weapons.

Harrier III: Even though the V/STOL version of the Joint Strike Fighter (JSF) is intended to replace the Harrier in USMC, RAF and RN service, McDonnell Douglas (Boeing since August 1997) and British Aerospace (BAE Systems since December 1999) have been quietly working on a third generation 'Harrier III' in case the JSF doesn't eventuate. Their studies are based on a development of the AV-8B Plus.

ZD406, one of 49 Harrier GR.5/5As converted to FLIR equipped GR.7 standards. Since 1994 the GR.7 has been the only single seat Harrier variant in RAF service.

The Harrier GR.7 is similar to the USMC's AV-8B Night Attack model. It has been delivered in both new build and converted forms and entered RAF service in 1990. This pair is operated by 4 Squadron RAF.

HARRIER II

Powerplant: AV-8B - one 21,450lb (95.4kN) Rolls-Royce F402-RR-406A (Pegasus 11 Mk.21) or 23,800lb (105.9kN) F402-RR-408A (Pegasus 11 Mk.61) vectored thrust turbofan. GR.5/7 - 21,550lb (95.8kN) Pegasus 11 Mk.105. Internal fuel capacity 969imp gal (1,164 USgal/4,406 l) in five fuselage and two integral wing tanks; four 250imp gal (300 USgal/1,136 l) underwing drop tanks.

Dimensions: AV-8B - wing span 30ft 4in (9.25m); length 46ft 4in (14.12m); height 11ft 8in (3.56m); wing area 230sq ft (21.4m^2) or 243sq ft (22.6m^2) with larger leading edge extensions. GR.7 - length 47ft 8in (14.53m). AV-8B Plus - length 47ft 9in (14.55m).

Weights: Typical operating empty 13,970-15,705lb (6,337-7,124kg); max takeoff (STO) 31,000-32,000lb (14,062-14,515kg); max takeoff (VTO) 19,180-20,753lb (8,700-9,413kg).

Armament: AV-8B - one optional 25mm five barrel cannon in ventral pod; seven stores pylons for max 13,234lb (6,003kg) ordnance with -408A engine. GR.7 - optional two 25mm cannon in ventral pod; nine stores pylons for max 10,800lb (4,900kg) ordnance.

Performance: AV-8B - max speed 585kt (1,083km/h) at sea level; initial climb 14,715ft (4,485m)/min; combat radius (hi-lo-hi) with 3,500lb (1,588kg) bomb load and drop tanks 595nm (1,102km); max ferry range 1,965nm (3,640km). AV-8B Plus - radius of action 200nm (370km) close air support lo-lo-lo, 400nm (742km) interdiction or 540nm (1,000km) anti-ship mission.

Harriers For Two

Even though work on a two seat operational trainer version of the P.1127 had been studied in parallel with development of the single seater in 1959-60, it would not be until April 1969 that the first aircraft flew (under the designation Harrier T.2), some 16 months after the Harrier GR.1 had taken to the air.

A requirement for a two seat version of the P.1127 capable of performing not only the training role but also delivering the weapons planned for the single seater was issued in February 1961 but withdrawn later in the same year. This was due to official interest shifting to the supersonic P.1154 project and continued development of the Kestrel evaluation aircraft.

Interest in a P.1127 two seater was renewed in 1964 but mainly as a precursor to developing a training version of the P.1154. When that was cancelled shortly afterwards, the idea once again lapsed but was revived when it was decided to go ahead with a full operational version of the Kestrel for the RAF.

Finally, in late 1966, a contract for the construction of a pair of prototype two seaters was issued to Hawker Siddeley.

The earlier investigations into a trainer version of the P.1127 had examined various tandem and side-by-side seating arrangements including an interesting one nicknamed the 'tuning fork' with two separate forward fuselages with individual cockpits.

The RAF at the time preferred side-by-side seating in its trainers but this proved to be impractical in the P.1127 as major structural changes would have been necessary along with the need to 'spread' the engine intakes further apart, introducing unacceptable inefficiencies and complications to the air inlet ducting system.

Developing a two seat version of a fighter is usually a relatively straight forward affair but the P.1127's VTOL capabilities meant that a delicate balance existed and had to be maintained. The second cockpit could not cause changes to the aircraft's centre of gravity, which had to be kept

Development of a two seat Harrier began in 1966 and the first example flew in April 1969. XW927 was the second of two Harrier T.2As delivered to the RAF in 1972.

Hawker Siddeley built a two seater for demonstrations and tests as the Mk.52. It is photographed here over Rio de Janeiro during a 1973 demonstration tour of Brazil.

within the limits imposed by the centre of thrust. Weight was also a critical issue in an aircraft designed to takeoff and land vertically.

It was therefore quickly realised that a tandem seating arrangement was the only possibility. To achieve the aircraft's design aims (for use as a conversion trainer with full weapons capability and to maintain the highest possible commonality with the single seater), Hawker Siddeley's designers split the single seater's forward fuselage immediately aft of the cockpit and inserted a new 47in (1.19m) section containing the second cockpit, which was mounted 18in (46cm) higher.

As the new cockpit was also a few inches further aft than the original, some equipment had to be relocated into a fairing on the upper fuselage behind it, while a completely new one piece and sideways opening canopy covered both seats.

To counter the destabilising effect of the longer forward fuselage and its reduced weathercock stability, the fin was moved 33.3in (85cm) further aft and was made 11in (28cm) taller by installing a new base. A ventral fin was also fitted and the wing remained as per the single seater. To maintain centre of gravity, a 6ft (1.83m) longer tail cone was incorporated to carry 170lb (77kg) of ballast. The ballast was removed if the aircraft was flown as a single seater.

The first development Harrier T.2 (XW174) flew on 24 April 1969 but was lost in early June following a fuel system fault. The second aircraft (XW175) flew on 14 July 1969. Although the single seater's superb flying qualities were retained, it was discovered the two seater's directional and weathercock stability had some problems in certain flight regimes despite the increase in fin area which had been incorporated.

After much testing, a fin and rudder which was a further 18in (46cm) taller was fitted on all but the earliest production Harrier two seaters and was subsequently retrofitted to those which had been built before the modification had been finalised. Although it had been found that a 23in (58cm) taller fin provided the best aerodynamic solution to the problem, concerns about its structural integrity led to installation of the slightly shorter fin, this proving to be a fair compromise.

But even that was not the end of the story for the Harrier trainer's fin. When some later aircraft were fitted with a radar warning receiver (RWR) antenna on the leading edge of the fin (as on the GR.3), the extra surface area it created made for too much stability at low angles of attack and the fin height had to be reduced by fitting a standard GR.3 unit to the trainer's taller fin base.

The Harrier T.2 weighed about 1,400lb (635kg) more than the GR.1 single seater and despite the design and conceptual difficulties which had to be overcome, the level of structural, systems, ground support equipment and ground crew training commonality between the two versions was high. As per the initial requirement, combat capability was retained.

The first of the initial batch of production Harrier T.2s for the RAF (XW264) flew on 3 October 1969 and first deliveries were made to the Harrier Operational Conversion Unit (No 233 OCU) at Wittering in July 1970.

T.2: The initial two seat Harrier for the RAF: 19,000lb (84.5kN) thrust Pegasus 6 Mk.101; maximum rolling takeoff weight 24,000lb (10,886kg); first flight (development aircraft) 24 April 1969; first flight (production aircraft) 3 October 1969; first delivery July 1970; final delivery January 1972; 12 built of which nine converted to T.2A and then to T.4.

T.2A: Similar to the T.2 but with a 20,500lb (91.2kN) thrust Pegasus 10 Mk.102; two built at the end of the initial production batch and delivered to the RAF between February and July 1972; both later converted to T.4.

T.4: Trainer version for the Harrier GR.3 with 21,500lb (95.6kN) thrust Pegasus 11 Mk.103 and 26,300lb (11,930kg) maximum takeoff weight, most with RWR on fin and lengthened LRMTS (Laser Rangefinder and Marked Target Seeker) nose. First flight (XW933) May 1973; 14 new aircraft built in four batches and delivered to the RAF between August 1973 and February 1984; also nine T.2/As converted to T.4 standards and seven T.4s later converted to T.8s.

T.4A: Designation applied to T.4s used only as conversion trainers and therefore lacking the LRMTS nose; production details included in T.4 (above).

T.4N: Similar to T.4A (without LRMTS nose) but for Royal Navy land based training; three built and delivered to the RN between September 1983 and January 1984. These were the first Harrier two seaters built specifically for the RN, conversion training of Sea Harrier pilots had previously been carried out in RAF aircraft.

A Spanish Navy TAV-8S alongside an AV-8S well illustrates some of the major differences between the single and two seat first generation Harriers.

T.6: 1987 designation of a planned night attack training version of the T.4 with night vision equipment for training Harrier GR.7 pilots. Not built and superceded by the Harrier T.10.

T.8: The Royal Navy's trainer for the Sea Harrier F/A.2 with a 21,500lb (95.6kN) thrust Pegasus 11 Mk.106 engine and front cockpit similar to the F/A.2 including multifunction and headup displays (HUD) but lacking radar; capable of carrying AIM-9 Sidewinder acquisition rounds. Seven converted from T.4s and delivered from May 1995.

T.10: The RAF's 'Harrier II' trainer for the Harrier GR.7 powered by a 21,550lb (95.8kN) thrust Pegasus 11 Mk.105; airframe similar to the USMC's TAV-8B (see below) but with full operational/weapons capability and the GR.7's cockpit with digital moving map display, avionics, FLIR and systems; eight underwing hardpoints. Fourteen were ordered in February 1990 but this was reduced to 13 due to budgetary constraints. First flight (ZH653) 7 April 1994; first delivery to No 20 (Reserve) Squadron 30 January 1995; final delivery (ZH665) 26 October 1995 as the last Harrier II to emerge from the British assembly line.

Mk.52: Designation applied to the privately funded Hawker Siddeley/British Aerospace demonstrator aircraft; similar to the Harrier T.2A powered by Pegasus Mk.102 and later Mk.103 engine; carried dual civil registration and military serial G-VTOL/ZA250, the latter to allow the carriage of weapons. Used for numerous demonstrations to potential export customers plus various tests and trials. First flight 16 September 1971, retired December 1988.

Mk.54: UK designation for US Marine Corps TAV-8A Harriers.

Mk.58: UK designation for Spanish Navy TAV-8S/VAE.1 Matador two seaters.

T.60: Four trainers for the Indian Navy mechanically similar to the RN's T.4N but equipped with the Sea Harrier FRS.51's avionics and cockpit but with radar deleted. The first order was placed in 1979 and deliveries began in 1983.

VAAC: The second Harrier T.2 (XW175) has spent its entire life being used for operational tests and trials and in 1983 was modified by the Cranfield Institute of Technology for the testing of new concepts in V/STOL aircraft

Second generation trainer - a single seat AV-8B and two seat TAV-8B display their differences.

control systems. After being upgraded to T.4A standards, the aircraft's rear cockpit was rebuilt to incorporate VAAC (Vectored thrust Aircraft Active Control) technology and as a result became the world's first fly-by-wire V/STOL, aircraft.

Features included a re-programmable digital flight control computer with the standard Harrier control system and performance parameters (control inputs, reaction control system, flaps, throttle, nozzle angles etc) digitally copied. The aircraft was flown via two control sticks - one for speed and one for direction- with the conventional throttle control lever eliminated.

In 2000, and operated by the UK Defence Evaluation and Research Agency (DERA), the VAAC Harrier began flying as part of the Joint Strike Fighter (JSF) programme, employed on risk reduction work on STOVL flight control development and to investigate design options for the STOVL version of the JSF.

TAV-8A: Eight 'first generation' Harrier two seaters delivered to the US Marine Corps; called Harrier Mk.54 by the British. Powered by a 21,500lb (95.6kN) thrust Pegasus 11 Mk.103 (US military designation F402-RR-402), the TAV-8B was similar to the RAF's T.4A but incorporated US operational equipment and upgrades similar to those installed in the AV-8A.

The USMC TAV-8As were delivered after the single seat AV-8As, the first aircraft (BuAer 159378) flying on 16 July 1975. Deliveries began in October 1975 and had been completed by the end of 1976. The USMC's Harrier training squadron (VMAT-203 at Cherry Point, North Carolina) operated the TAV-8A until November 1987.

BuAer 162747 was the first of 24 TAV-8B Harrier IIs delivered to the USMC. It recorded its maiden flight in October 1986.

TAV-8S: The Spanish Navy's two TAV-8S two seaters were similar to the USMC's TAV-8As apart from different radios to ensure compatibility with the service's helicopters. The two aircraft were delivered in February and July 1976; alternative designations were the local VAE.1 Matador and British Harrier Mk.58.

TAV-8B Harrier II: The second generation Harrier trainer for the US Marine Corps combined the new wing of the single seat AV-8B with a tandem two seat forward fuselage which although conceptually similar to that developed for the early model trainers, was of a largely new design. Overall length was increased by 3ft 11in (1.19m) compared to the AV-8B, the fin was 1ft 5in (43cm) taller and had a slightly increased chord, and the extended and ballasted tail cone of the earlier trainers was not fitted.

Although USMC TAV-8Bs featured the single seat Harrier II's digital cockpit and new systems, they were not combat capable and had only two underwing hardpoints for drop tanks or training weapons. The RAF's equivalent Harrier T.10, by comparison, was fitted with eight underwing hardpoints and was fully combat capable. The TAV-8B was initially powered by the 21,450lb (95.4kN) thrust F402-RR-406A (Pegasus 11 Mk.21) and subsequently the 23,800lb (105.8kN) thrust F402-RR-408A or Pegasus 11 Mk.61 as installed in later AV-8Bs.

The first of 24 TAV-8Bs for the USMC (BuAer 162747) was also the 65th Harrier II to emerge from the McDonnell Douglas line and first flew on 21 October 1986. Deliveries to the USMC Harrier training squadron VMAT-203 began in July 1987.

The TAV-8B designation was also applied to two aircraft delivered to the Italian Navy as part of a 1989 order which included 16 AV-8Bs. All were supplied by McDonnell Douglas. The Spanish Navy received a single new build TAV-8B from the same source.

The RAF's Harrier II trainer is the T.10. First flown in April 1994, 13 were delivered, the last in October 1995 as the final second generation Harrier to roll off the British assembly line.

Harrier Operators

Royal Air Force

The RAF took delivery of its first Harrier GR.1 on 18 April 1969, the aircraft handed over to No 233 Operational Conversion Unit (OCU) on that date. The first operational squadron to covert to the aircraft was No 1 at Wittering, Cambridgeshire in June 1969, followed by No 4 at Wildenrath, Germany in April 1970, No 20 at Wildenrath in December 1970 and No 3 at Laarbruch, Germany in January 1972.

The RAF maintained a Harrier GR.1/GR.3 presence at Belize (the former British Honduras) almost unbroken from 1975 to 1993, No 1417 Flight stationed there to counter the threat of invasion from Guatemala.

These four units have remained the operators of the RAF's Harrier force in all its versions since then, except for No 20 which switched to the Jaguar in 1977 and Tornados later on. It returned to the V/STOL fold in September 1992, reconstituted as No 20 (Reserve) Squadron as the Harrier training unit. Essentially a renaming of 233 OCU, the squadron is based at Wittering.

The Harrier GR.5 entered RAF service in July 1987 and the GR.7 in July 1990.

The two RAF Germany squadrons transferred to Cottesmore in Rutland during 1999 in anticipation of the implementation of the Joint Force Harrier concept on 1 April 2000. Announced in the 1998 UK Defence Strategic Review (originally as 'Joint Force 2000'), this initiative sees the RAF's Harrier GR.7s and the Royal Navy's Sea Harrier F/A.2s operating under a single command.

The force is part of the newly established 3 Group within a restructured Strike Command, the Group also responsible for the operation of Nimrod maritime patrol aircraft and search and rescue helicopters. It is regarded as an important element of Britain's shift to expeditionary air power and the ability to provide greater flexibility.

JFH will see RAF Harrier GR.7s regularly operating from the Royal Navy's *Invincible* class carriers alongside their naval brethren. A typical shipboard Harrier complement will be eight GR.7s and eight F/A.2s. By the end of 2000, all three RAF Harrier operational squadrons were based at Cottesmore and were to be joined by the RN's Sea Harrier units in 2003. Only No 20(R) Squadron remained at the RAF's traditional British Harrier base, Wittering.

All the threes. A trio of Harrier GR.3s of 3 Squadron RAF. From top to bottom they are XV738, XZ134 and XV781.

Two AV-8B Plus Harrier IIs of USMC squadron VMA-542. Note the chaff/flare dispensers on the upper rear fuselage and the lengthened ram air intake at the base of the fin.

The concept of joint RAF/RN Harrier operation is not entirely new, as the two services operated their aircraft side by side during Operation Corporate, the battle to regain the Falkland Islands from Argentina in April-June 1982. A total of 12 Harrier GR.3s was deployed to the Falklands during the conflict, flying under the auspices of No 1 Squadron. They were used very effectively in the ground attack and anti shipping roles, the 150 sorties flown mainly from the carrier HMS *Hermes* but also from a rudimentary forward operating base at San Carlos.

Four Harrier GR.3s were lost during the conflict, three of them to Argentinean ground fire and one following an engine failure during a vertical landing. A further four had been despatched to the Falklands but arrived after the ceasefire on 14 June 1982. The RAF established a 1 Squadron detachment at Port Stanley (later renamed 1453 Flight) to help ensure the security of the islands, this remaining in place until May 1985 when Phantoms were sent as replacements .

Since then, RAF second generation Harriers have been regularly involved in NATO peacekeeping operations including over Bosnia, patrolling the 'no fly' zone in Iraq and Kosovo operations in 1999.

The RAF received 84 Harrier GR.1s, 40 GR.3s (plus 61 converted from GR.1s), 43 GR.5s, 19 GR.5As, 34 GR.7s (plus 49 converted from GR.5s) and 41 two seaters of various models.

Royal Navy

The Sea Harrier FRS.1 entered service with the Royal Navy Fleet Air Arm on 18 June 1979 when XZ 451 was handed over to the Sea Harrier Intensive Trials Unit (subsequently No 700A Naval Air Squadron) based at RNAS Yeovilton in Somerset. It was renamed 899 Squadron in March 1980, established as primarily a shore based training unit with the occasional embarkation undertaken.

The first front line squadron to receive the aircraft was No 800 in March 1980 followed by No 801 in January 1981. All three were and remain based at Yeovilton with deployments aboard the purpose built 'Harrier Carriers' HMS *Invincible*, *Ark Royal* and *Illustrious*. During the Falklands campaign of April-June 1982, 800 Squadron operated from the refitted HMS *Hermes* (with ski ramp) and 801 from *Invincible*.

A fourth squadron - No 809 - existed only between April and December in 1982 to provide attrition replacements for aircraft and pilots deployed in the Falklands campaign.

The other three squadrons re-equipped with the Sea Harrier F/A.2 (initially conversions from existing airframes) in 1994-95.

The Sea Harrier FRS.1 won international fame during the Falklands War, the aircraft of Nos 800 and 801 Squadrons between them flying 2,376 sorties and downing 23 Argentinean aircraft for no losses in air-to-air combat. Of the six Sea Harrier losses suffered during the campaign, two were due to ground fire and four to accidents.

The Sea Harrier achieved true air superiority in the Falklands, to the extent that Argentinean aircraft crews became reluctant to deliberately engage it in combat. There were several keys to its success, notably the very high sortie rate achieved by a small force of only about 20 aircraft at any one time (turnaround times of just 10 minutes were achieved), and the availability of the advanced AIM-9L version of the Sidewinder air-to-air missile. This had not been cleared for use on the Sea Harrier when the British Task Force was committed to retake the Falklands but an emergency clearance was given within a few days, an alacrity unthinkable in peacetime.

RN Sea Harrier FRS.1s found themselves in action again over Bosnia in 1993-94 before being withdrawn from service in March 1995.

From April 2000, the service's F/A.2s became part of the Joint Force Harrier concept with the RAF's GR.7s, as described above.

Sea Harrier deliveries to the RN were 57 FRS.1s, 18 F/A.2s (plus 34 converted from FRS.1s), three new T.4Ns and seven T.8s converted from RAF T.4s.

United States Marine Corps

The USMC received the first of an eventual 102 first generation AV-8A Harriers (plus eight TAV-8A trainers) in January 1971, the aircraft and their engines manufactured in the UK despite Hawker Siddeley and Rolls-Royce having signed licence production agreements with McDonnell Douglas and Pratt & Whitney. The ordering of the aircraft in relatively small annual batches made it more economical for them to be imported from Britain, although this changed later when the AV-8B Harrier II was developed.

The initial operator was Marine Attack Squadron VMA-513 based at MCAS Beaufort, South Carolina. It and the two other original operational

The Indian Navy received 23 Sea Harrier FRS.51s from January 1983 along with four T.60 trainers.

units (VMA-542 and VMA-231) plus the training squadron VMAT-203 were all based at MCAS Cherry Point, North Carolina by 1977 and were joined by a new unit (VMA-331) in early 1985.

The first McDonnell Douglas/British Aerospace AV-8B Harrier II was delivered to the USMC in January 1984, the type replacing the earlier Harrier plus the A-4 Skyhawk in several squadrons. Aircraft from the 167th in 1989 were completed to Night Attack standard with FLIR and pilot night vision goggles.

Total USMC procurement has been 232 AV-8Bs, 30 AV-8B Plus (with another 72 converted from the basic model) and 24 TAV-8Bs. Those AV-8Bs being remanufactured to AV-8B Plus standards have new BuAer numbers, and about 40 had been delivered by late 2000. The first new build AV-8B Plus flew in September 1992.

In late 2000, the AV-8B equipped seven Marine Attack squadrons, VMA-211, 214, 311 and 513 at Yuma, Arizona with the Night Attack version and VMA-223, 231 and 542 at Cherry Point with the basic and Plus models. The training squadron (VMAT-203) operated AV-8Bs and TAV-8Bs out of Cherry Point.

The USMC was seeking funding for additional AV-8B Plus aircraft in 2000, while the fleet was grounded in July of that year following a crash resulting from a bearing failure in the aircraft's F402-RR-408 engine. A progressive modification programme was due to be completed by April 2001.

The AV-8B's combat debut was in the 1991 Gulf War, 86 USMC aircraft from five units flying 3,380 missions and 4,112 combat hours from an unprepared airfield at Tanajib in Saudi Arabia and from the USS *Nassau*. Five were lost to Iraqi surface-to-air missiles but the deployment of the aircraft was successful.

After the conflict, US commander General Norman Schwarzkopf named the AV-8B as one of the seven weapons which had made a significant contribution to a quick and decisive victory. Only three aircraft were named in this commendation, the Harrier, F-117 Nighthawk and AH-64 Apache attack helicopter.

Most of the Italian Navy's 16 Harrier II single seaters were assembled locally by Alenia but its two TAV-8Bs were built in the USA.

Indian Navy

The only export customer for the Sea Harrier, Indian interest in the aircraft began in July 1972 when Hawker Siddeley's two seater demonstrator G-VTOL/ZA250 flew from the carrier INS *Vikrant*. It would be more than seven years before an order was placed, a December 1979 contract covering an initial six Sea Harrier FRS.51s and two T.60 trainers, the latter basically

similar to the Royal Navy's T.4N. The Sea Harrier replaced the veteran Hawker Sea Hawk in Indian service.

Subsequent Indian Navy orders placed in November 1985 and August 1986 brought the FRS.51 total up to 23 aircraft along with four T.60s. A further two ex RAF T.4s were purchased in 1996 as attrition replacements.

The first FRS.51 flew on 6 August 1982 (the 34th Sea Harrier off the line) and the first aircraft was handed over to the Indian Navy on 27 January 1983. Deliveries of the initial batch had been completed by March 1984. Operational service was with No 300 Squadron aboard the *Vikrant* (which was fitted with a 9.75deg ski ramp), this joined in 1987 by the Falklands War veteran HMS *Hermes*, renamed INS *Viraat* in Indian service. No 551 Squadron is the Indian Navy's Harrier pilot conversion unit

Vikrant was decommissioned in 1996, ending speculation of a further purchase of Harriers as with only one carrier available, the existing fleet was deemed sufficient. Various upgrades have been studied, including one to modify the aircraft to F/A.2 standards, but the US Government's refusal to issue an export licence for the AIM-20 AMRAAM missile ended that idea.

Spain has been a major Harrier customer, ordering both first and second generation models for its navy. This is the first EAV-8B (or VA.2 Matador II), delivered in October 1987.

Italian Navy

The *Marina Militare Italia's* interest in the Harrier began in 1967 with a flight demonstration aboard the anti submarine helicopter carrier *Andrea Doria*, but it would be another 22 years before an order was placed.

The main problem was inter-service rivalry and a 1937 Italian law which prohibited the MMI from operating fixed wing aircraft, that to be the domain of the air force. The navy was subsequently able to fly helicopters, but only because they did not exist when the legislation was introduced and were therefore not covered by it.

Various proposals for the MMI to buy Harriers were promulgated over the years but the service forced the issue in 1983 with the launch of the helicopter carrier *Giuseppe Garibaldi*. This incorporated a 6.5deg ski ramp on the end of a full length flight deck and the intention was clear. Officially, the ramp was described as being a device to 'protect the flight deck from excessive spray'!

A change to the law was proposed in 1985 but after much air force versus navy squabbling, it wasn't until January 1989 that a new law was passed, allowing aircraft with a maximum weight of over 1,500kg (3,307lb) to fly with the MMI.

The MMI had meanwhile been carrying out a lengthy evaluation of the

Sea Harrier and AV-8B Harrier II, with an initial order for a pair of TAV-8B two seaters placed in May 1989 with McDonnell Douglas. This was quickly followed with a contract for 16 AV-8B Plus aircraft.

The two seaters and first three single seaters were built in the USA but the remaining 13 were delivered in kit form for assembly in Italy by Alenia. Other Italian companies were also involved through offset work: Aerea (pylons), Breda (cannon), Fiat Avia (engine components) and Magnaghi (hydraulics). An option was placed on a further eight aircraft but this had not been taken up by the time the AV-8B production line closed.

Deliveries began in April 1994, initially to Marine Corps Air Station Cherry Point for training. The first landing on the *Giuseppe Garibaldi* was recorded in November 1994, more than a decade after the ship had been launched. The first Italian assembled Harrier rolled off the line in late 1995 and both of the TAV-8Bs have subsequently been re-engined with more powerful F402-RR-408 engines.

Italy's Harriers saw early combat in January 1995 when the US built AV-8Bs operated by 1 *Gruppo Aereo* (normally based at Grottaglie) provided fire support for UN troops evacuating from Somalia. They flew over 100 combat hours using 25mm cannon and rocket pods and achieved 100 per cent availability during the campaign.

In late 2000, the MMI was looking to acquire an additional six or seven remanufactured AV-8Bs to equip both the *Giuseppe Garibaldi* and a new carrier which is due to enter service in 2006-2007. The existing aircraft are being upgraded to carry the Raytheon AIM-120 AMRAAM and Boeing JDAM GPS guided bombs.

Spanish Navy

The *Arma Aérea de la Armada* ordered six single seat and a pair of two seat Harriers in August 1973, despite relations between Spain and Britain being somewhat strained at the time due to a dispute over Gibralter. In 1972, the British Government (led by Harold Wilson) had cancelled a Spanish order for four frigates which were to be built in British shipyards.

Despite this, Hawker Siddeley test pilot John Farley had been able to demonstrate a Harrier GR.3 aboard the Spanish helicopter carrier *Dédalo* (the former USS *Cabot*) in August 1972 and the decision was made to purchase the aircraft.

Some internal Spanish political issues had to be sorted out first, notably the fact that the use of fixed wing, carrier based aircraft by the Spanish Navy was forbidden by law. This was circumvented by arguing that as the Harrier did not takeoff and land conventionally, it was really a fixed wing helicopter!

Spain wanted the aircraft badly but because of the difficulties with Britain, the order had to placed through the US Marine Corps which added them to its own order and then resold them to Spain. The single seaters were designated VA.1 Matador by the Spanish, AV-8S by the USA and Harrier Mk.55 by the British; the two seaters were VAE.1, TAV-8S and Mk.58, respectively.

The aircraft were basically similar to the USMC's AV-8A and TAV-8A except for different radios to ensure compatibility with Spanish Navy helicopters.

Deliveries of the first batch of Matadors began in November 1975 and the operational squadron, *Escuadrilla* 008 was commissioned in September 1976 in Florida after training for its pilots had been undertaken in the USA. When embarked on the *Dédalo*, the squadron became the world's first Harrier unit to operate regularly at sea. A further five single seaters were ordered in 1977, mainly as attrition replacements and delivered from June 1980.

The Matadors were armed with Sidewinder AAMs and primarily used in the air defence role with a secondary but little used close air support capability. The *Dédalo* was replaced in service by the new and Brazilian built carrier *Príncipe de Asturias*, launched in 1982 and commissioned six years later. Of 16,700 tonnes displacement, the ship was fitted with a 12deg ski ramp and although intended mainly for the new AV-8B Harrier IIs ordered by Spain, it also briefly embarked the earlier aircraft.

In 1992, seven surplus AV-8Ss and two TAV-8Ss were ordered by the Royal Thai Navy (see below).

The Spanish Navy became the first international customer for the AV-8B Harrier II in March 1983 when it ordered 12 as the EAV-8B or VA.2 Matador II. Deliveries began in October 1987 and all had been handed over by the end of 1989.

A further eight were ordered in EAV-8B Plus configuration in March 1993 along with a single TAV-8B with deliveries starting in 1996. At the same time, the decision was made to upgrade the 11 surviving earlier aircraft to 'Plus' standards, this enabling them to carry four AMRAAM missiles, although by mid 2000 testing to expand the AV-8B's carriage envelope to an operationally acceptable standard had not been completed.

Funding restrictions had also slowed the upgrade of earlier aircraft with only four committed for modification by July 2000 and the last two scheduled for redelivery in June and July 2003.

Spain's EAV-8Bs were involved in Operation Deny Flight, supporting NATO operations over Bosnia.

Royal Thai Navy

The Spanish Navy sold seven AV-8S and two TAV-8S Matadors to the Royal Thai Navy in a $US70m deal signed in early 1992. After refurbishing, they were delivered in 1996 and assigned to 301 Squadron based at U-Tapao. Pilot training began in the USA in 1995.

The aircraft were subsequently embarked on the new Spanish built 11,500 tonne carrier RTNS *Chakri Naruebet*, delivered in August 1997 and equipped with a 12deg ski ramp. Several surplus USMC AV-8A/Cs were also purchased from storage for spares.

Thailand's operation of the Harrier has had its problems with the aircraft grounded in mid 1997 (and operation of the carrier curtailed) due to a chronic lack of funds.

The Royal Thai Navy received seven ex Spanish AV-8S and two TAV-8S Matadors in 1996, but budgetary problems have restricted their operation.

Serial Numbers

Royal Air Force
P.1127: XP831; XP836; XP972; XP976; XP980; XP984; total 6.
Kestrel FGA.1: XS688-XS696; total 9.
Harrier GR.1: XV276-XV281; XV738-XV762; XV776-XV810; XW630; XW916-XW924; XW763-XW770; total 84. Conversions: 40 GR.1 to GR.1A and 61 GR.1/1A to GR.3.
Harrier T.2: XW174-XW175; XW264-XW272; XW925; total 12. Conversions: 9 T.2 to T.2A and then T.4.
Harrier T.2A: XW926-XW927; total 2. Conversions: both to T.4.
Harrier GR.3: XZ128-XZ139; XZ963-XZ973; XZ987-999; ZD667-670; total 40. Additional 61 converted from GR.1/1A.
Harrier T.4: XW933-XW934; XZ145-XZ147; XZ445; ZB600-ZB603; ZD990-ZD993; total 14. Conversions: 7 to T.8.
Harrier Mk.52: ZA250/G-VTOL; Hawker Siddeley demonstrator.
Harrier GR.5: ZD318-ZD319; ZD320-ZD330; ZD345-ZD355; ZD375-ZD380; ZD400-ZD412; total 43. Conversions: 33 to GR.7.
Harrier GR.5A: ZD430-ZD438; ZD461-ZD470; total 19. Conversions: 16 to GR.7.
Harrier GR.7: ZG471-ZG480; ZG500-ZG512; ZG530-ZG533; ZG856-ZG862; total 34. Additional 49 converted from GR.5/5A.
Harrier T.10: ZH653-ZH665; total 13.

Royal Navy
Sea Harrier FRS.1: XZ438-440; XZ450-XZ460; XZ491-XZ500; ZA174-ZA177; ZA190-ZA195; ZD578-ZD582; ZD607-ZD615; ZE690-ZE698; total 57. Conversions: 34 to F/A.2.
Sea Harrier F/A.2: ZH796-813; total 18. Additional 34 converted from FRS.1.
Harrier T.4N: ZB604-ZB606; total 3.
Harrier T.8: 7 conversions from T.4 ZB603-ZB605 and ZD990-ZD993.

United States Marine Corps
AV-8A: BuAer 158384-158395; 158694-158711; 158948-158977; 159230-159259; 159366-159377; total 102. Conversions: 47 to AV-8C and 2 to YAV-8B.
TAV-8A: BuAer 159378-159385; total 8.
YAV-8B: 2 conversions from AV-8A 158394 and 158395.
AV-8B: BuAer 161396-161399; 161573-161584; 162068-162088; 162721-162746; 162942-162962; 162964-162970; 162972-162973; 163176-163179; 163181-163185; 163187-163190; 163192-163195; 163197-163201; 163203-163206; 163419-163426; 163514-163519; 163659-163690; 163852-163855; 163862-163883; 164115-164121; 164123-164135; 164139-164154; 164543-164547; total 232. Note: completed as AV-8B(NA) from 163853. Conversions: 72 to AV-8B Plus planned.
AV-8B Plus: New build - BuAer 164548-164571; 165001-165006; total 30. Remanufactured with new serial numbers - BuAer 165305-165312; 165354-165357; 165380-165391; 165397-165398; 165417-165423; 165451-165454; 165566-165597; total 72.
TAV-8B: BuAer 162747; 162963; 162971; 163180; 163186; 163191; 163196; 163202; 163207; 163856-163861; 164113-164114; 164122; 164136-164138; 164540-164542; total 24.

Indian Navy
Sea Harrier FRS.51: IN 601-IN 623; total 23.
Harrier T.60: IN 651-IN 654; total 4.

Spanish Navy
AV-8S Matador: 008-1/008-6; 008-9/008-13 (BuAer 159557-159562, 161174-161178); total 11.
TAV-8S: 008-7/008-8 (BuAer 159563-159564); total 2.
EAV-8B: 01-901/01-912 (BuAer 163010-163021); total 12.
EAV-8B Plus: 01-914/01-922 (BuAer 165028-165035); total 9.
TAV-8B: 01-923 (BuAer 165036); total 1.

Italian Navy
AV-8B Plus: MM7199-MM7201; MM7212-MM7224 (BuAer 164563-164565, 165007-165019); total 16.
TAV-8B: MM55032-MM55033 (BuAer 164136-164137); total 2.

Harrier Production Summary
(new airframes)

P.1127	6
Kestrel GR.1	9
Harrier GR.1	84
Harrier T.2	12
Harrier T.2A	2
Harrier GR.3	40
Harrier T.4	14
Harrier T.4N	3
Harrier Mk.52	1
Harrier GR.5	43
Harrier GR.5A	19
Harrier GR.7	34
Harrier T.10	13
Sea Harrier FRS.1	57
Sea Harrier FRS.51	23
Sea Harrier F/A.2	18
Harrier T.60	4
AV-8A Harrier	102
TAV-8A Harrier	8
AV-8S Matador	11
TAV-8S	2
AV-8B	232
EAV-8B	12
AV-8B Plus	46
EAV-8B Plus	9
TAV-8B	27
Total	**831**

Summary: 15 prototypes/development, 237 'first generation' single seaters, 98 Sea Harriers, 395 Harrier II single seaters and 86 two seaters of all versions.